TEACH YOURSELF TO
BLUES
GUITAR

By Dave Rubin

To access video visit:
www.halleonard.com/mylibrary

Enter Code
4641-1492-7432-1036

ISBN 978-1-4950-3005-5

HAL•LEONARD®

Table of Contents

Introduction

Welcome. You are about to enter the dangerous world of blues guitar. Dangerous? Yes, because exposure to the most powerful and emotional music may indeed be "dangerous," as playing it can become a lifelong obsession. I mean no disrespect to other forms of great music and am only being half facetious about the inherent dangers of playing blues guitar, including getting poisoned in a juke joint in Mississippi for messing with another man's woman!

The good news is you do not have to go to the crossroads and swap your soul to the devil for the requisite blues guitar skills. They exist right before you and will be introduced clearly and logically chapter by chapter. Familiarity with the basic open-position major and minor chords, major and minor barre chords, a smattering of theory, and at least the root position of the minor pentatonic scale will be useful.

The melodic roots of the blues go back to West Africa and beyond. My theory is they originate in the Middle East whence the melancholy, minor-key tonalities made their way to Africa via caravans and trading, at which point they were played on one-string "diddley bows" and gourd proto-banjos. The harmony, or chord progressions, may be traced back to the 15th-century folk music of the British Isles. Magically, almost cosmically, the two blended together on plantations in the South sometime after the Civil War, becoming the glorious cultural achievement of African-Americans following Emancipation. By the late 1800s, "Frankie and Albert" and "Joe Turner Blues" were making the rounds in the South as the first recognizable rumblings of the 12-bar blues. Concurrently, guitars left behind by Union soldiers after the Civil War were being picked up by nascent blues musicians even as banjos and harmonicas were still ruling the day as the original accompaniment instruments.

W.C. Handy began copyrighting and publishing blues songs in 1912 with the obscure "Memphis Blues." His "St. Louis Blues" in 1914, however, is a landmark and classic still performed today. In 1920, Mamie Smith recorded the first commercially successful blues with "Crazy Blues." It was played by musicians with Dixieland jazz experience and, like much of the backing for the "Classic Women Blues Singers" of the 1920s, it had a sophisticated, urban sound with piano and horns minus guitars.

In 1926, Texas legend Lemon Henry "Blind Lemon" Jefferson cut "Booster Blues" among others, and the era of wildly influential country and Delta blues guitar commenced commercially. Charlie Patton, Eddie "Son" House, Tommy Johnson, Lonnie Johnson, and later Robert Johnson rambled with the acoustic music up to just before the start of WWII. In the early 1940s, the pioneering and revolutionary electric guitar mastery of Texas legend T-Bone Walker would spark the development of postwar electric blues in his home state, along with Chicago, the West Coast, and other urban centers. Acoustic country blues would be relegated to the dustbin of history until the blues revival of the early 1960s when both it and electric blues crossed over to the hip college audience. At the same time, British blues and rock guitarists were reimagining Chicago and Texas blues, ramping it up with energy and fat, expressive distortion while "turning around" the music and sending it back to its homeland where young American guitarists and fans would enthusiastically embrace it. Through the ups and downs and vagaries of popular taste, the music endures as the greatest artistic expression to inspire, soothe, nourish, and stimulate.

The only thing left to do now is to start right in on Chapter 1 and have fun while taking this "amazing journey" to the blues.

Dave Rubin

NYC

About the Video

To access all of the videos that accompany this book, simply go to **www.halleonard.com/mylibrary** and enter the code found on page 1. The music examples that include video are marked with an icon throughout the book.

Dedication and Acknowledgments

This book is dedicated to all who would search deep in their souls for the ultimate "blue note." Special thanks to Jeff Schroedl, an excellent blues guitarist in his own right, and all at Hal Leonard for 25 years of support and friendship.

Chapter 1
What Is a 12-Bar Blues?

The 12-bar blues is the most common blues chord progression, though there are 8-bar blues as well as 16- and 24-bar blues, to a lesser extent. In its simplest form, 12-bar blues contain the first, fourth, and fifth chords—referred to as I, IV, and V—from the major scale of whichever of the 12 keys is chosen. For example, in the key of A, they would be A, D, and E. In the key of E, they would be E, A, and B, etc.

The Slow Change

There are only two basic variations of 12-bar blues. The first is known as the "slow change" because it consists of four measures, or bars, of the I chord preceding the IV chord in measure five. **Fig. 1** shows the "slow change" in the key of A.

Fig. 1

Chord:	A	A	A	A	D	D	A	A	E	D	A	E
Bar:	1	2	3	4	5	6	7	8	9	10	11	12

The Fast Change

The second variation is called the "fast change" where the forward momentum from the I to the IV chord occurs in measure 2, as seen in **Fig. 2**. Take care to notice how both progressions are exactly the same after measure 2. As a general rule, perhaps curiously, the "fast change" appears more in slow blues, while the "slow change" appears more in up tempo blues. However, there are many examples of the opposite, and it is a subjective decision as to which one is chosen.

Fig. 2

Chord:	A	D	A	A	D	D	A	A	E	D	A	E
Bar:	1	2	3	4	5	6	7	8	9	10	11	12

Note that it's also common to remain on the I chord for bar 12 as well, instead of moving to the V chord. This is particularly true of minor blues, which we'll look at later on.

The following chapters will explain how to easily and quickly translate this information into playing the "blues approved," "real deal," and "down and dirty" blues guitar as performed by the greats.

Chapter 2
Boogie Patterns – The Heart of Blues Rhythm Guitar

Boogie patterns are derived from boogie woogie music as played on pianos and guitars. Piano boogie woogie often involves "walking bass lines" of eight bass notes per measure. Guitar boogie woogie more typically consists of two or three bass-string notes played in conjunction with an open-string or barred "pedal tone" (see "Barre Chord Boogie Patterns," which follows) and are referred to as "cut boogie" patterns. The main value of cut boogie patterns is displayed in their characteristic ability to provide rhythm and harmony simultaneously—a great virtue particularly if one is the only guitarist in a group. Robert Johnson popularized the technique with "Sweet Home Chicago" (1936), while Jimmy Reed in the 1950s built virtually his entire career on cut boogie patterns, in the process influencing generations of blues and rock guitarists.

Open-Position Boogie Patterns

Fig. 3 contains the most basic example in the key of A, as it is the easiest one to learn because it does not require a barre-chord fingering. Notice how the I (A), IV (D), and V (E) chord changes incorporate strings 5 (A), 4 (D), and 6 (E) open as the root notes, respectively. **Performance Tip:** Use the index and ring fingers, respectively, for the fretted notes in each chord change.

Fig. 3

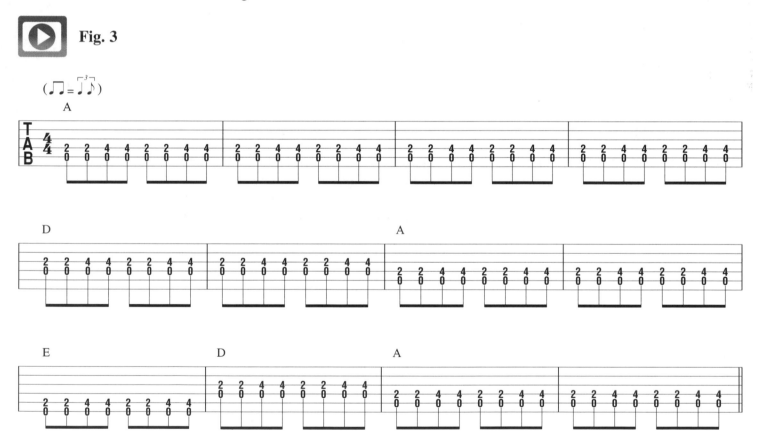

Shuffle Feel

You may have noticed the (♪♪ = ♪♪) symbol at the beginning of the previous example. This indicates a *shuffle feel* or *swing feel* and lets you know that the eighth notes should have a lopsided feel, in which the first in each beat is longer than the second. This should almost be considered the default in blues unless otherwise stated.

There are a number of bass-string embellishments that add variety to standard boogie blues progressions or songs. **Fig. 4** is a classic favored by guitarists as well as piano players, as it contributes a noticeable boost of momentum with minimal effort. **Performance Tip:** Leave the index finger on string 4 for the I chord, string 3 for the IV chord, and string 5 for the V chord while playing the two-note bass-string lick on strings 5, 4, and 6 with the middle and ring fingers, respectively.

▶ **Fig. 4**

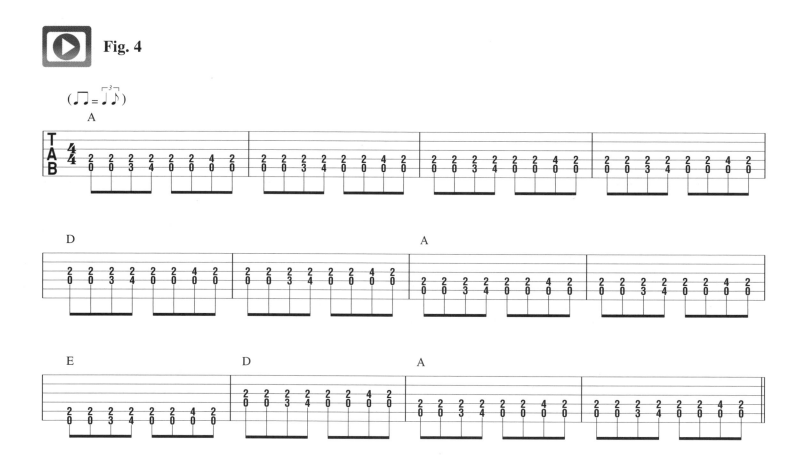

Fig. 5 extends the harmony to imply A7, D7, and E7 chords. It also moves a "step" closer to full piano walking bass lines. **Performance Tip:** Utilize the index, ring, pinky, and ring fingers in sequence for the fretted notes in each chord change.

Fig. 5

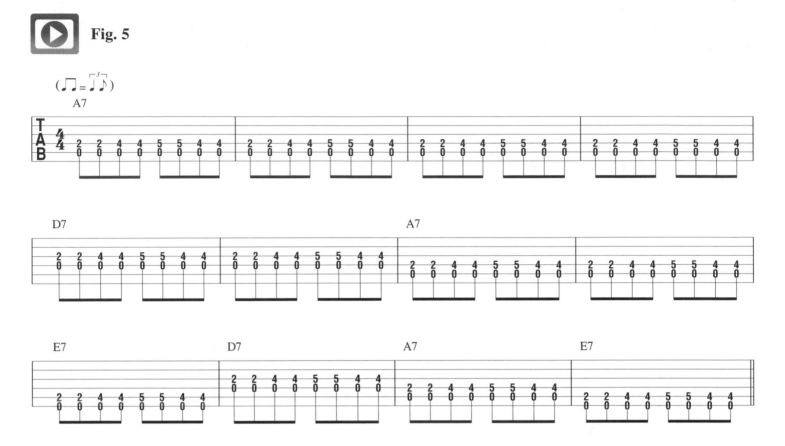

Barre-Chord Boogie Patterns

The popular key of A has been the logical choice so far to begin learning cut boogie patterns, as it does not necessitate a barre chord for any of the three chord changes. The key of E, however, is equally, if not more, favored among blues guitarists and is a required aspect of the blues guitar curriculum.

Fig. 6 incorporates two forms already shown while introducing the basic cut boogie barre-chord pattern for the V (B) chord. Be sure to notice how the patterns for the IV (A) chord as well as the V consist of the most basic cut boogie forms. Besides making it easy to learn the first blues barre-chord form, it also illustrates the concept of *not* having each I, IV, and V pattern be *exactly* the same. One of the tiresome complaints from non-fans is "the blues sounds all alike." Of course it is not true, but varying similar patterns and forms will go a long ways to adding welcome variety. Observe the appearance of a classic blues turnaround ending on the V (B) chord in measure 12, which is far hipper than just repeating the boogie pattern for the V chord.

Turnarounds may appear in the last two measures of a blues verse or progression. In a 12-bar blues, this would mean bars 11 and 12. A turnaround literally reverses direction of the verse, sending it back to the I chord in the next verse by ending on the V chord.

Performance Tip: Even though only two strings are struck in measure 9 over the V chord, many guitarists are more comfortable barring straight across all six strings with their index finger while accessing the note on string 4 at fret 4 with the ring finger and the note at fret 6 with the pinky. Access the bluesy seventh-chord voicing in measure 12 of the turnaround with the middle, index, and ring fingers, low to high.

Fig. 6

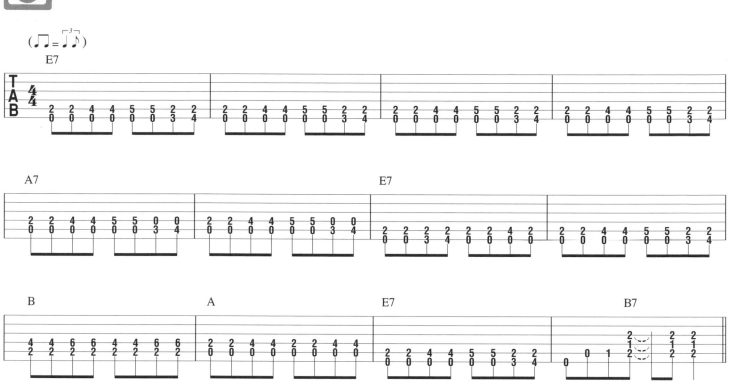

The key of G is also a common blues key while affording barre-chord fret positions conducive to 14-fret acoustic guitars, along with virtually all electric guitars.

In **Fig. 7**, the barre-chord form shown for the V (B) chord in **Fig. 6** is utilized as a moveable form from fret 3 (G) to fret 8 (C) and fret 10 (D) on strings 6 and 5. **Performance Tip:** Technically, these fingerings will apply to all barre-chord boogie patterns, including barring across all six (or five) strings with the index finger. Observe a variation in measure 12 during the turnaround where "resolution" to the V chord (D7) is reached from one-half step above via the E♭7 chord.

Fig. 7

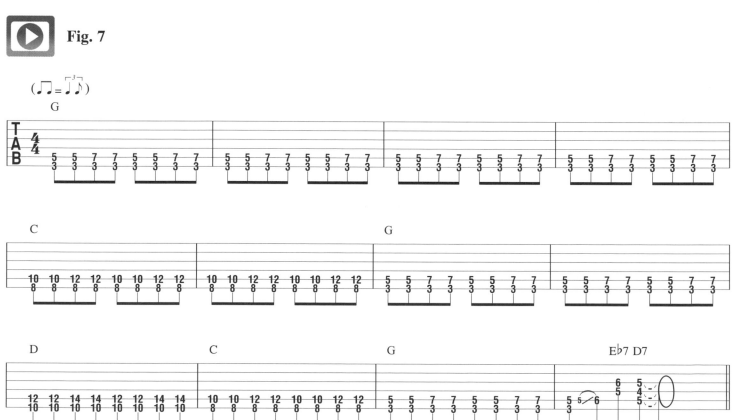

Fig. 8 contains the alternative barre-chord boogie patterns for the IV (C) and V (D) chords, voiced on strings 5 and 4 rather than 6 and 5. Observe the "walk up" to the V chord (D7) similar to **Fig. 6**. **Performance Tip:** Index finger strength, as far as holding down two or more strings at the same time, is paramount to blues guitar. The best way to achieve it is literally by playing barre chords as an exercise, like going to the gym!

▶ **Fig. 8**

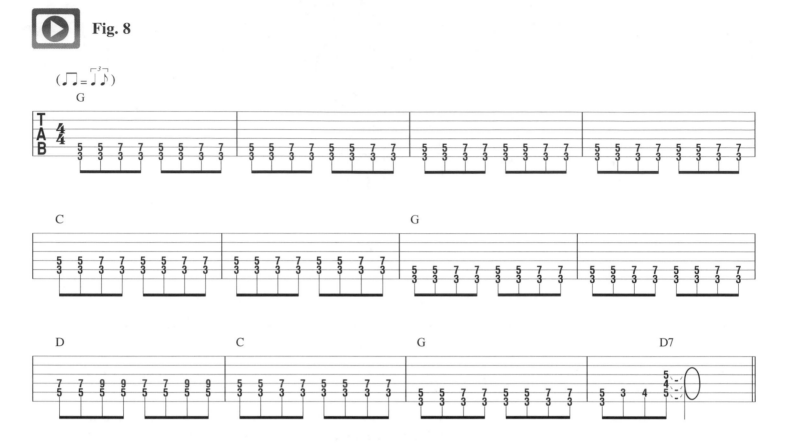

Fig. 9 includes the same two-note bass-string embellishment as seen in **Fig. 4**. In the manner of blues rock, measure 12 features "power chords," also known as "5ths." **Performance Tip:** The embellishments should be accessed with the pinky finger. The power chords in measure 12 are traditionally played with the index and ring fingers, low to high.

▶ **Fig. 9**

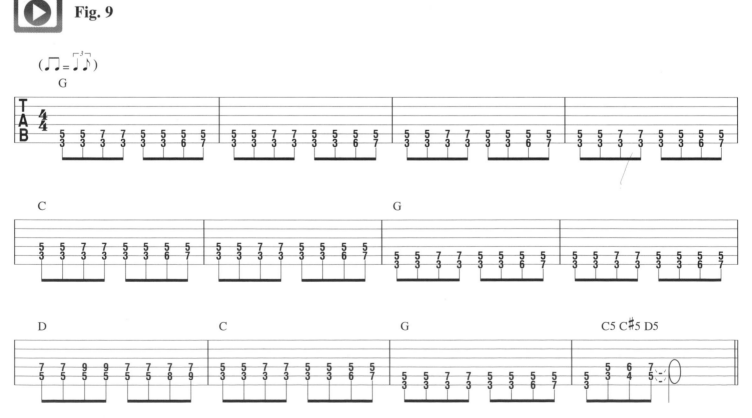

Chapter 3
Learning to Play Rhythm with Open-Position Seventh Chords

In addition to boogie patterns, strummed seventh chords, theoretically known as *dominant seventh chords*, are likewise of prime importance in the playing of blues songs. Open seventh-chord forms are not as versatile as barre-chord forms, but they do afford access to the popular blues keys of E, A, D, and G. **Performance Tip:** Chord frames in **Fig. 10** will provide the fingerings, also known as "voicings," for the following musical figures.

Fig. 10

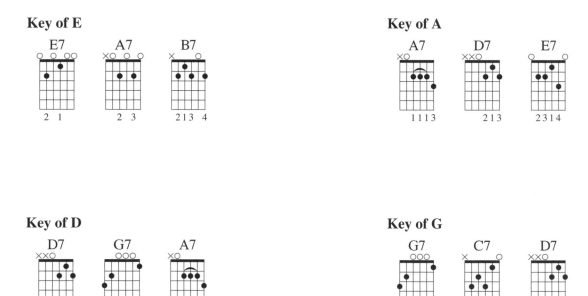

Key of E

Fig. 11 is a basic, "fast change" 12-bar blues in the key of E with open seventh chords. **Performance Tip:** Note how measures 11 and 12 are divided into two chords of two beats each in what is a standard chord turnaround of I–IV–I–V chords.

Fig. 11

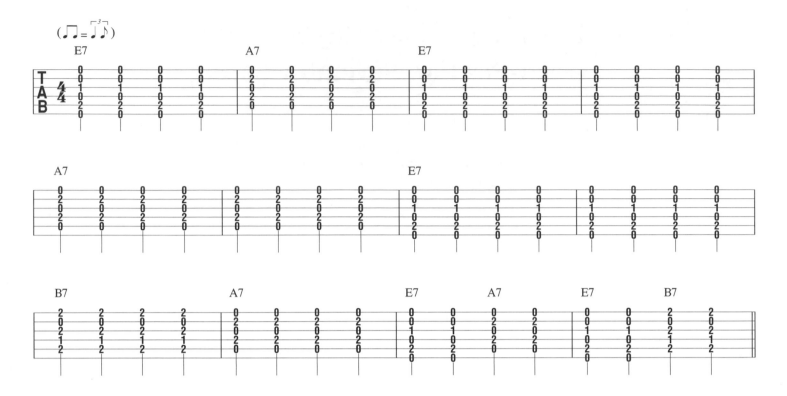

Key of A

Fig. 12 is the same as **Fig. 11**, but in the key of A. (Note that, in the music for **Figs. 12**, **13**, and **14**, quarter-note strums are shown, as in **Fig. 11**, but in the video, I play varied rhythms for a more musical effect.)

 Fig. 12

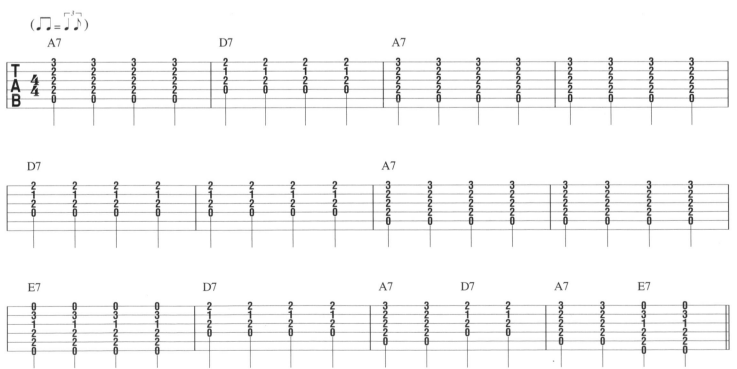

Key of D

Fig. 13 is the same as **Fig. 11**, but in the key of D.

 Fig. 13

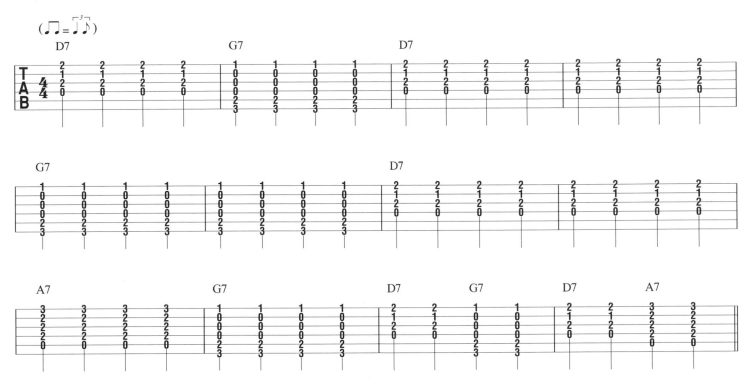

Key of G

Fig. 14 is the same as **Fig. 11**, but in the key of G.

 Fig. 14

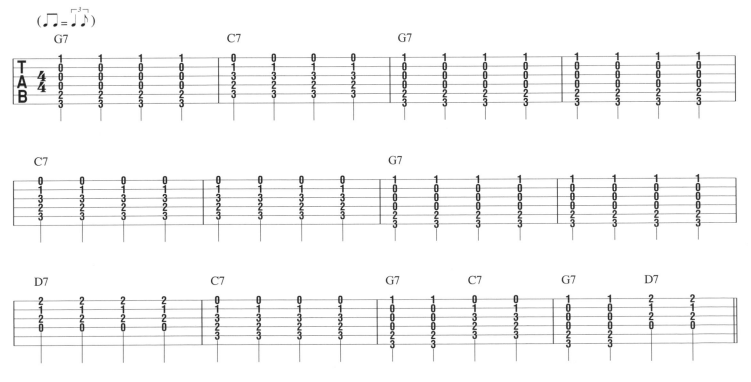

Chapter 4
Rhythm Guitar with Barred Dominant and Minor Chords

As you probably know, barre chords allow access to all 12 keys simply by moving the appropriate chord shapes up and down the fingerboard, the same as with the barre-chord boogie patterns. For all the examples in this chapter, quarter-note strums are shown to demonstrate the chord shapes used, but again, I'll vary the rhythms in the video demonstrations.

Barred Dominant Chords

Fig. 15 is a "slow change" in the key of E utilizing barred seventh chords "voiced" (fingered) with the root note on string 6 for each of the I, IV, and V chords. **Performance Tip:** As with virtually all barre chords, it is strongly recommended to keep the thumb directly behind the barring index finger on the back of the neck for maximum pressure with the least effort.

Fig. 15

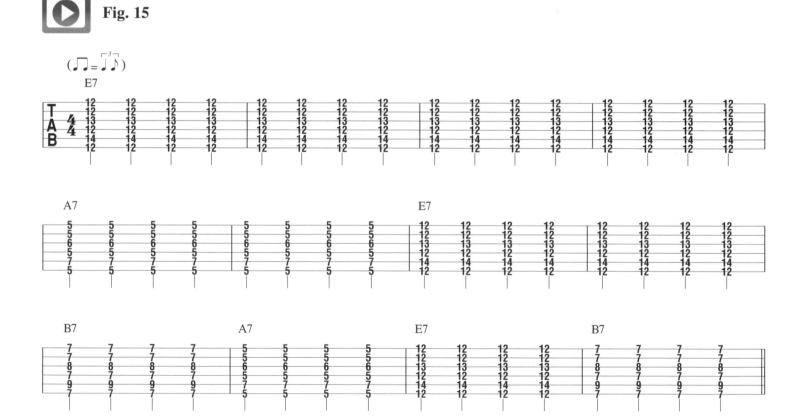

Fig. 16 introduces barred seventh chords with the root note on string 5, using a "fast change" progression in the key of E. Notice how a change of voicings gives the effect that more is happening than actually is, for variety sake. **Performance Tip:** In measures 6, 7, and 12, you could keep your barred index finger across all six strings for efficiency, as the chords are at the same fret positions, respectively.

Fig. 16

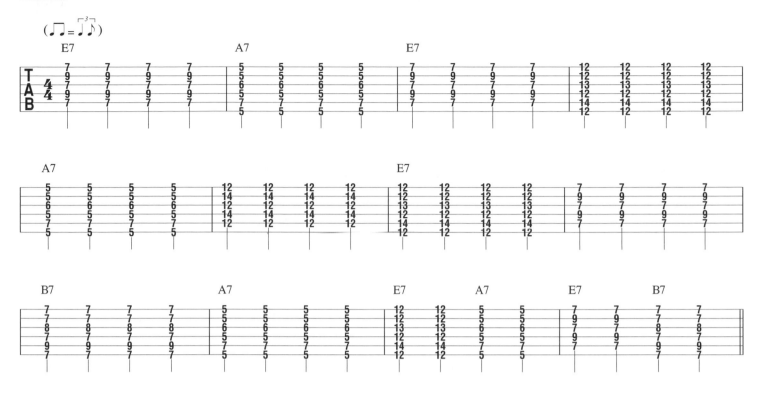

Fig. 17, with the "fast change" in the key of A, contains a seventh-chord variation illustrating a prime virtue of smart blues rhythm guitar. Measures 4, 8, 11, and 12 (A7 chord) and measure 6 (D7 chord), respectively, have a subtly different voicing that functions to increase forward momentum by adding a note from the previous voicing one octave higher. Be aware how, theoretically, the harmony has not changed. In addition, using the new form on the A7 in measures 1 and 12 serves to make a smoother transition to the D7 and E7 chords. **Performance Tip:** Access the higher note with the pinky finger.

Fig. 17

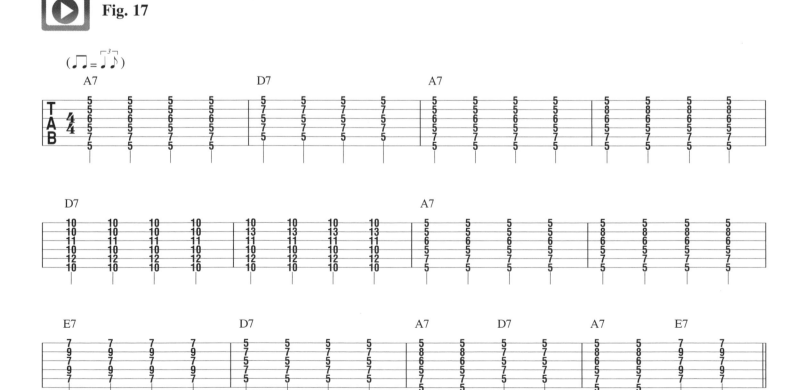

The hip ninth chord voicing shown in **Fig. 18** is an important staple of blues rhythm guitar, as well as R&B, funk, and jazz. Though not technically a full barre chord, it does incorporate a partial barre. **Performance Tip:** Until the fingering becomes second nature and a reflex, try laying your ring finger across strings 3, 2, and 1 first before placing down the index and middle fingers.

 Fig. 18

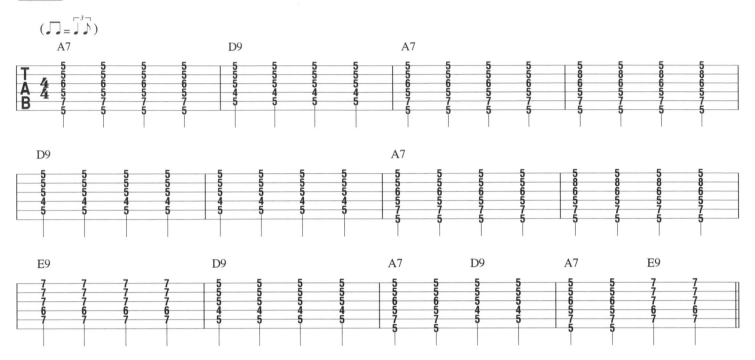

Minor Blues

Fig. 19 contains the first variation of the three most commonly found forms in minor-key blues songs. The I chord, usually noted in lower case as "i," is the only minor chord in the progression. **Performance Tip:** As with many basic blues progressions involving barre chords, it is most efficient to leave the barre index finger in place across all six strings, even for five-string voicings.

 Fig. 19

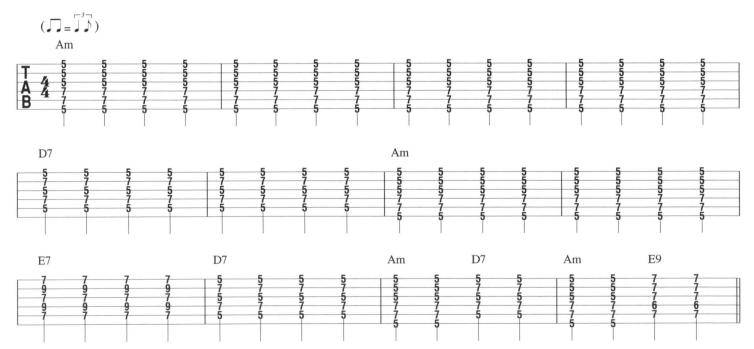

The second 12-bar minor blues variation, shown in **Fig. 20**, has minor i (Am) and iv (Dm) chords. However, E7 concludes the progression in measure 12. **Performance Tip:** Observe the six-string root voicing for the E7 in measures 9 and 12 to help facilitate a smooth, efficient transition to the Dm in measure 10.

 Fig. 20

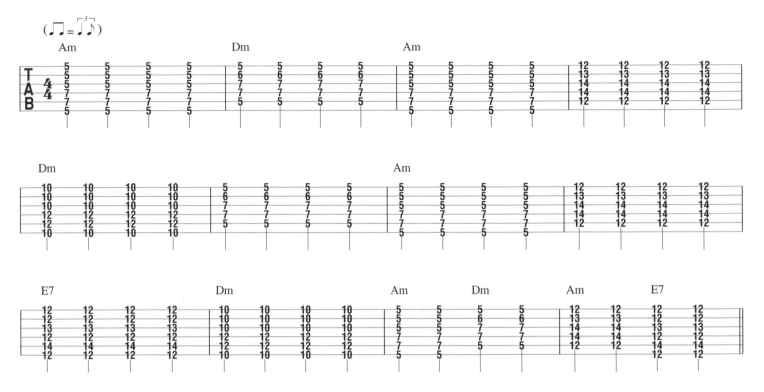

The third variation of 12-bar minor blues, shown in **Fig. 21**, employs minor voicings for i, iv, and v chords. It also features "jazzy" minor seventh (m7) chords for variety and to imply forward motion in the progression. **Performance Tip:** Measures 4, 6, and 11 only require lifting the appropriate fingers to access the m7 chords. Note how measure 12 in the turnaround typically contains an E7 chord for resolution, instead of the minor v.

 Fig. 21

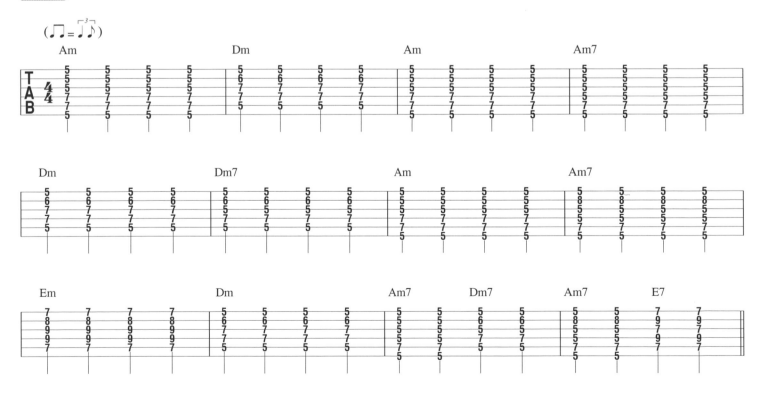

Chapter 5
8-Bar Blues

Most blues guitarists come to welcome a change from 12-bar to 8-bar blues. Classics abound, including "St. James Infirmary," "Nobody Knows You When You're Down and Out," "How Long, How Long Blues," "Key to the Highway," "It Hurts Me, Too," "You Got to Move," and "Trouble in Mind," among others.

Most Popular Form

Fig. 22 is likely the most popular classic 8-bar blues progression. Observe how the change from the I to the V chord instead of the IV chord in measure 2 gives a whole different cast to the flow of the progression. **Performance Tip:** In measure 7, leave the index finger on string 5 at fret 2 and then descend frets 5, 4, and 3 with the pinky, ring, and middle fingers for the turnaround.

▶ Fig. 22

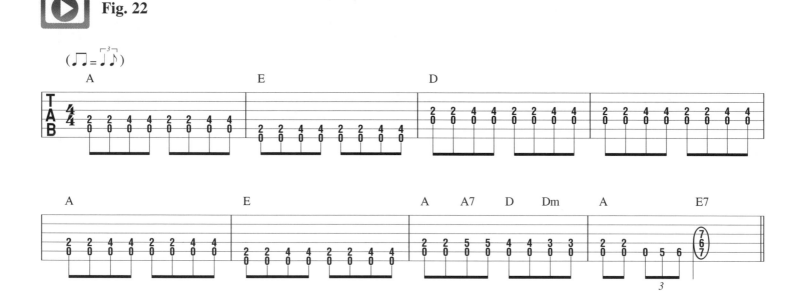

Substitute Chords

The VI (F♯) and II (B) chords are introduced in **Fig. 23** in a fashion similar to many 8-bar blues standards. They are theoretically referred to as "substitute chords" and add variety and richness to the progression, while opening up more melodic possibilities for the vocalist and soloists. **Performance Tip:** Note how four of the chords in measures 7 and 8 in the turnaround only require one strum each. Again, we'll simplify the notation to quarter-note rhythms for these next few examples, and I'll play some more varied rhythms on the video.

Fig. 23

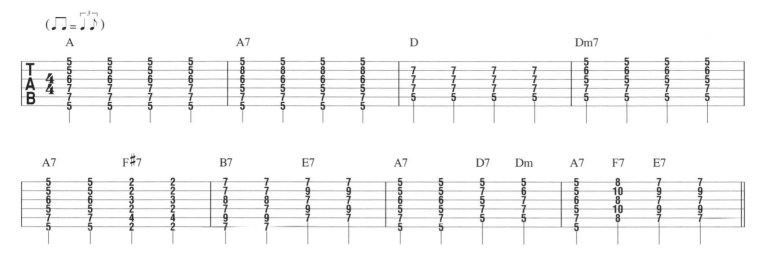

Uptown Blues

Fig. 24 takes a short subway trip "uptown" to the jazzy side of blues. Coincidentally, many jazz blues contain eight-measure verses combined with additional eight-measure sections. Check out how much more melodious and sophisticated the A6 sounds compared to an A7 as the I chord, for example. On top of that, be aware how the E+ in measure 8 creates even more anticipation and forward motion than a dominant seventh chord would in turning back around to the I chord for the next (implied) verse. **Performance Tip:** When switching from the A6 to D7 in measure 7, keep the ring and pinky fingers in place on strings 4 and 2, respectively, and just slide the index finger across fret 5 as a barre.

 Fig. 24

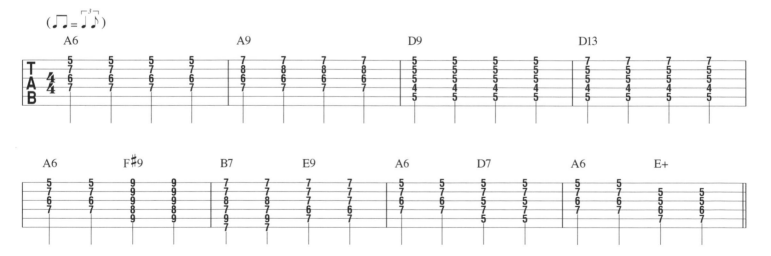

Minor 8-Bar Blues

Fig. 25 is based on "St. James Infirmary," which some believe to be one of the oldest blues songs. Minor in key, mournful, and melancholy, it is the essence of the earliest blues. **Performance Tip:** The move from Dm to A7 in measures 1 and 5 is easily accomplished by shifting the middle finger from string 3 to string 4 and sliding the ring finger down one fret on string 2.

 Fig. 25

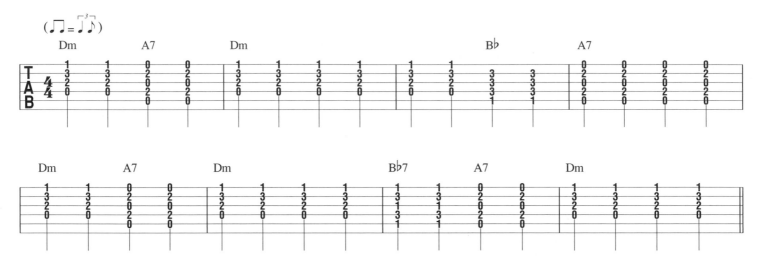

Chapter 6
Get Down with Bass-String Accompaniment Patterns

Minor Pentatonic Shuffle Patterns

As opposed to many other forms of music, blues guitarists often play cool bass-string lines in unison with the bassist. The most popular are derived from the minor pentatonic scale, as shown in **Fig. 26** in its root position in the key of A.

Fig. 26

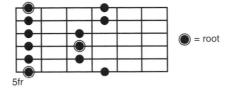

● = root

5fr

Fig. 27 contains a favorite pattern of Chicago blues musicians and, in particular, the reigning "King of Electric Blues," Buddy Guy. **Performance Tip:** Observe how the pattern for the I (A) chord change in measures 1–4 could be moved up the fingerboard to frets 10 and 12 to access the IV (D) and V (E) changes, respectively.

Fig. 27

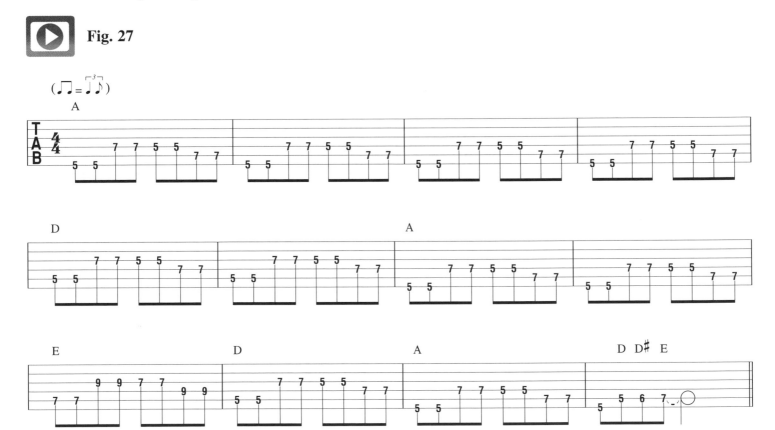

Freddie King incorporated patterns similar to **Fig. 28** in one of his classic instrumentals called "Heads Up." **Performance Tip:** Check out how it is essentially the reverse of **Fig. 27**.

 Fig. 28

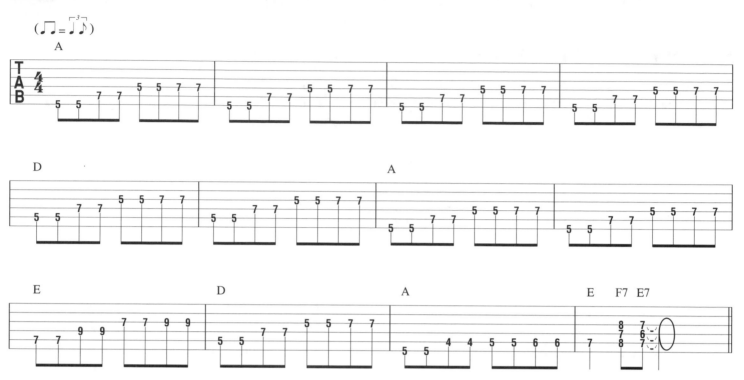

Minor Pentatonic Syncopated Pattern

The Allman Brothers employed patterns similar to **Fig. 29** for their version of the Elmore James classic "One Way Out." **Performance Tip:** As with the previous examples, only the index and ring fingers are required to access the patterns. However, the ring finger should be utilized as a small barre between beats 2 and 3 in each measure where notes are located on adjacent strings at fret 7 (for the I and IV chords) and fret 9 (for the V chord).

 Fig. 29

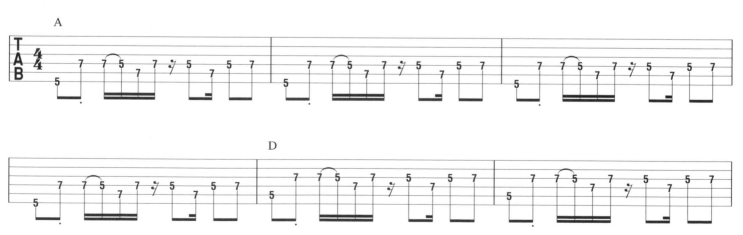

24

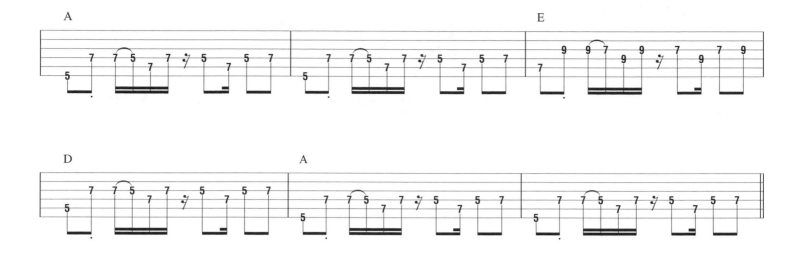

Chapter 7
Make It "Cry and Sing" by Soloing in the Blues Scale

Hot Licks

The *blues scale*, shown in the root position of A in **Fig. 30**, could be seen as adding a sixth note to the minor pentatonic scale. Like that most versatile rock and blues scale, it is moveable to all keys. This ♭5th (E♭) "blue note," found on strings 5 and 3, adds a tangy dissonance and is used effectively by blues guitarists to create musical, "bluesy" tension.

Fig. 30

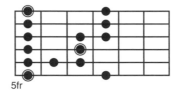

Fig. 31 could qualify as "Blues Lead Guitar 101" and has been played by countless blues guitarists too numerous to mention. However, a very short list of luminaries would include B.B. King, Otis Rush, Magic Sam, Buddy Guy, Eric Clapton, Jimi Hendrix, and Stevie Ray Vaughan. Be aware how the bend of the D note (one half step on string 3) accesses the "blue note" (E♭) in the most typical manner. **Performance Tip:** Bend the D with the ring finger backed up by the middle and index. Bend the G on string 2 with the pinky backed up by the ring, middle, and index fingers.

 Fig. 31

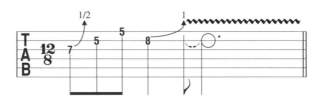

Jimmy Page, Eric Clapton, and Mick Taylor, among other British blues guitar heroes, were significantly influenced by the "Big Three" of Westside Chicago blues: Otis Rush, Magic Sam, and Buddy Guy. **Fig. 32** shows a favorite, slinky lick representative of the postwar electric blues masters. **Performance Tip:** On beat 1, bend the D note on string 3 with the ring finger backed up by the middle and index. Play the G note that follows on string 2 at fret 8 with the pinky.

 Fig. 32

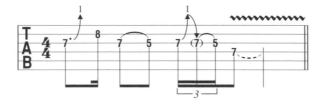

Freddie King, as well as others, often favored the dramatic descending lick in **Fig. 33**, as heard in his famous shuffle "Tore Down." **Performance Tip:** Bend the C note at fret 8 on string 1 with the pinky backed up by the ring, middle, and index fingers.

 Fig. 33

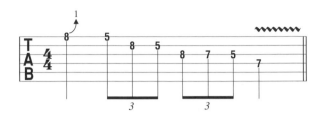

The extension position of the A blues scale shown in **Fig. 34**, commonly referred to as the "Albert King box" by many, is often employed to cop the famous licks of the "Velvet Bulldozer." Interestingly, the name of this scale position is a bit of a misnomer, as Albert himself did not make frequent use of it and played in a very unorthodox way: he flipped a right-handed guitar over and played it left-handed, so the thickest string was nearest the floor. He also tuned the guitar much lower than normal in a configuration that is still being debated. Nevertheless, the compact dimensions of the "Albert box" are extremely "finger friendly" while lending a myriad of potent licks.

Fig. 34

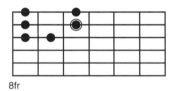

8fr

Fig. 35 is *the* classic Albert King lick and is versatile enough to be played over the I, IV, or V chords. **Performance Tip:** Although the bend from D to E on string 1 is usually played with the ring finger, it can also be done with the pinky, as demonstrated on the video. Vibrato the root note on string 2 at fret 10 by rapidly pulling *down* and pushing back up.

 Fig. 35

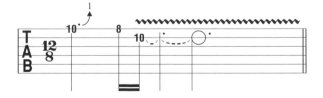

Fig. 36 employs the "blue note" as a *grace note*—that is, its function is to lead the listener directly to the 5th (E) that follows. **Performance Tip:** Play the E♭ with the index finger and hammer on to the E with the middle finger.

 Fig. 36

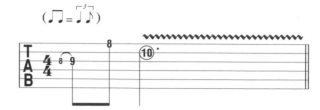

The "blue note" again functions as a grace note in **Fig. 37**, but this time via a half-step bend to it from the D note on string 1, followed by the release back to the D. Observe the way this lick ends on the G, rather than the root, which becomes a "leading tone" to encourage the ear to hear the next chord change. **Performance Tip:** Bend the D with the ring finger backed up by the middle and index.

 Fig. 37

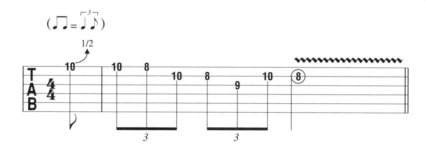

Fig. 38 contains the third most-played "blues box" at fret 12 in the key of A, though it's moveable to all other keys.

Fig. 38

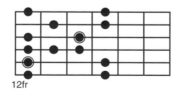

12fr

Fig. 39 has the iconic "train whistle lick," famous throughout the recorded history of the blues from Robert Johnson onward. This version maps out the basic move and notes. **Performance Tip:** Bend the C note on string 2 with the middle finger while accessing the E on string 1 with the index finger.

 Fig. 39

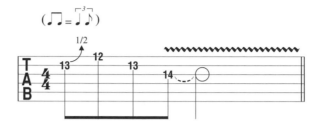

Fig. 40 features the full effect of the "train whistle" sound, so beloved by the prewar bluesman that had an affinity for the symbolic and literal meaning of trains rumbling through the Delta. Check out how the bend of a bluesy quarter step produces a gritty, throaty sound. **Performance Tip:** Low to high, use the middle and index fingers.

 Fig. 40

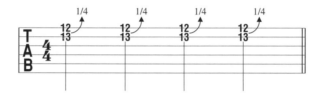

Jimmy Page, among his other peers, is partial to the "harmony bend" lick in **Fig. 41**. Note how the first two notes combined imply an A7 harmony. **Performance Tip:** Bend with the ring finger backed up by the middle and index fingers. Play the G note on string 1 at fret 15 with the pinky. Pull-off to the index finger, which should end up efficiently on the C note at fret 13, string 2.

 Fig. 41

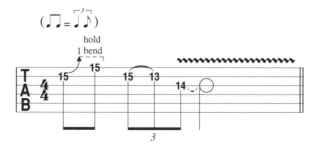

Hot Solos

Fig. 42 contains a slow blues solo in the classic post-B.B. King style. Pay attention to the rests, or musical spaces, as they are as crucial to the drama and emotional power of the solo as the actual notes. **Performance Tip:** It has been said by none other than the Rev. Billy "F" Gibbons that string bending separates the authentic blues guitarist from the poseur. This is particularly true regarding the critical quarter-step bends, which lose their effect if carelessly pushed up a half step.

Fig. 42

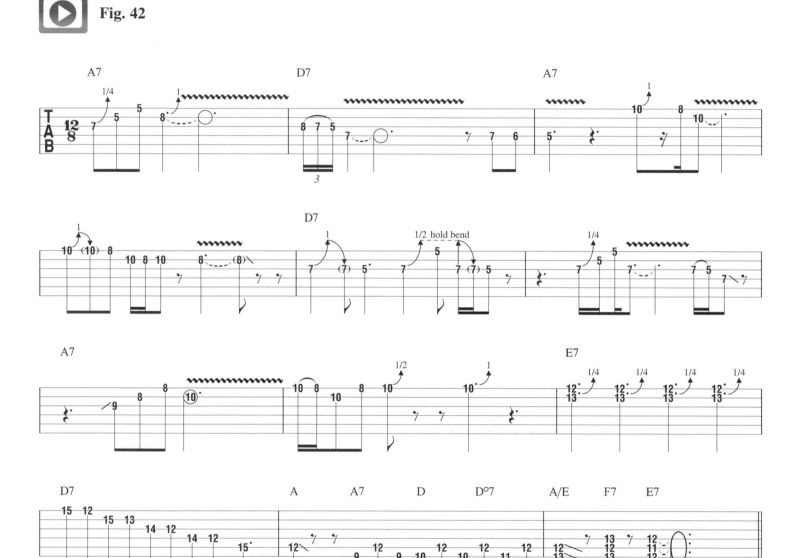

Otis Rush, Magic Sam, and Buddy Guy were the "Big Three" of Westside Chicago blues in the 1950s and 1960s. They took the pervasive influence of B.B. King and translated it into their own style with stinging licks, slinky vibrato, and fluid bends, as shown in **Fig. 43**. **Performance Tip:** The illustrious Mike Bloomfield advised to keep steady pressure on the string being bent and vibratoed in order to exact maximum sustain.

 Fig. 43

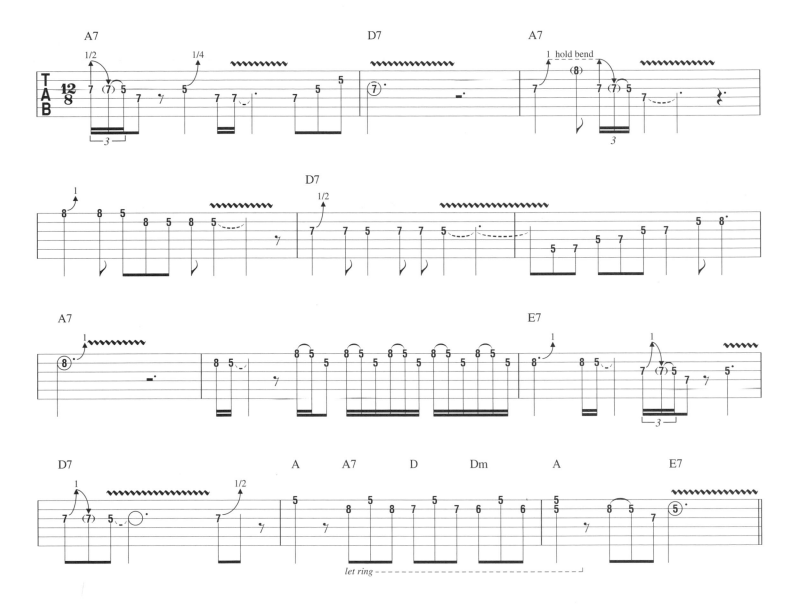

Eric Clapton in his Bluesbreakers and Cream days combined repeating triplets, sustained vibratoed notes, and tight clusters for exceptional dynamic and dramatic effect, similar to **Fig. 44**. **Performance Tip:** Though strict down/up alternate picking is generally considered the terrain of jazz and heavy metal guitarists, the technique is recommended at least for measures 10 and 11.

 Fig. 44

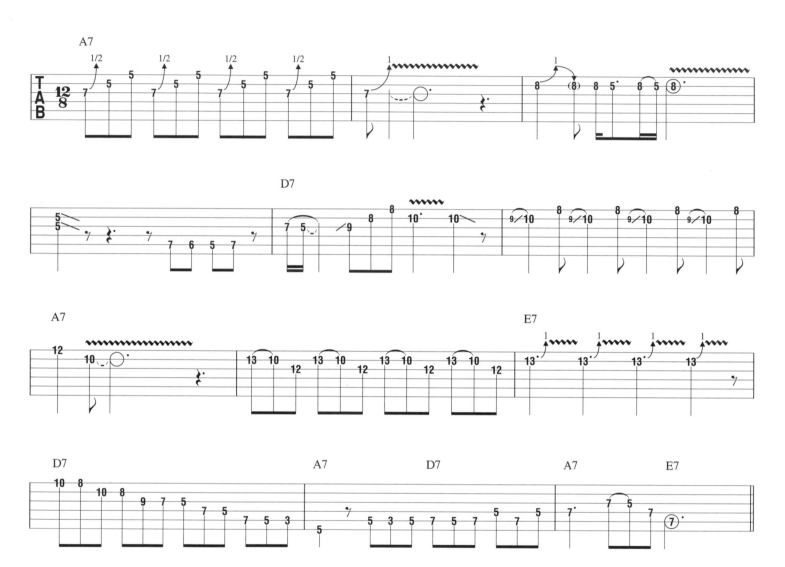

Chapter 8
Combining the Blues and Major Pentatonic Scales

The Composite Blues Scale

Blues guitarists have been "making hay" with the blues scale and its closely related cousin, the minor pentatonic scale, for 100 years and more. However, an advanced scale, known as the *composite blues scale*, has come into prominence in the post-WWII era thanks in large part to the late, great B.B. King. **Fig. 45** contains the A major pentatonic scale in the root position, while **Fig. 46** shows it in the far more advantageous *relative minor* pentatonic position. Though it would be the root position of the F♯ minor pentatonic if the key was F♯, in this context, it is the A major pentatonic scale. **Performance Tip:** The easy and accepted way to find your starting position, or "home base," with this exceptionally versatile scale is to think three frets below the root position of the major pentatonic scale. For example, in the key of A, the root position is at fret 5, and the relative minor pentatonic position is at fret 2. In the key of B, it would be frets 7 and 4, the key of C, frets 8 and 5, etc. Be aware how the key of G at fret 3 would necessitate utilizing the open position of the E minor pentatonic, or the octave position at fret 12.

Fig. 45

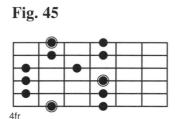

Fig. 46

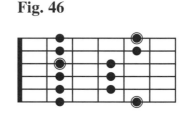

Fig. 47 shows the root position of the A composite blues scale. You should know that there are other combinations of notes which are also used, but this one is employed the most. **Performance Tip:** All four left-hand fingers should be utilized when accessing the scale for peak efficiency, though other choices are optional.

Fig. 47

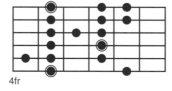

Composite Blues Extension Box

Fig. 48 presents the extension position, or "Albert King box," in the composite blues scale. **Performance Tip:** Low to high, use the index, middle, and ring fingers for the three notes on string 1.

Fig. 48

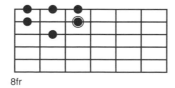

Eric Clapton Style

Though the "Father of Electric Blues," T-Bone Walker, utilized the composite blues scale previously (among others), B.B. King is generally credited as having brought it into popular usage. **Fig. 49** contains a solo similar to one Eric Clapton might play. **Performance Tip:** Though "Ol' Slowhand" is an avowed three-finger guitarist who rarely, if ever, uses his pinky when soloing, it is highly suggested to play the three-note combinations on string 2 in measures 4, 8, and 10, and string 1 in measure 7, with the pinky, ring, and index fingers.

 **Fig. 49**

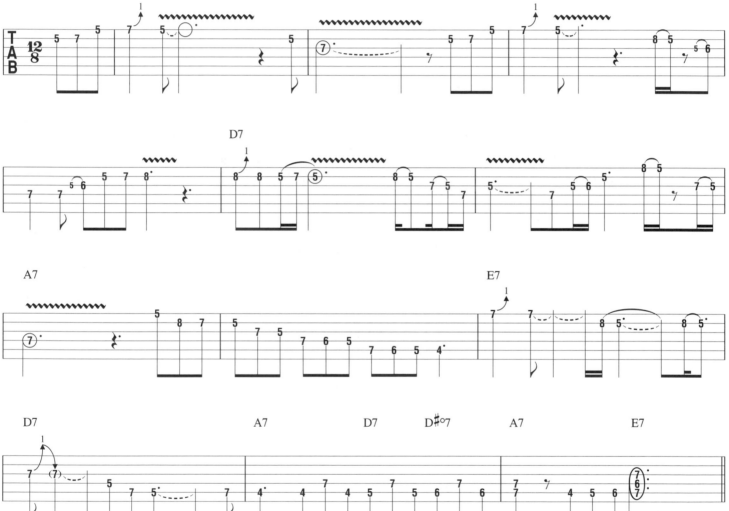

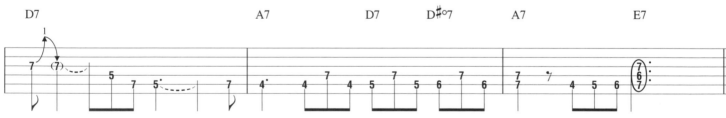

Texas Blues Style

Fig. 50 exhibits a tasty Texas flavor favored by Lone Star guitar slingers from Gatemouth Brown to Freddie King, Billy Gibbons, the late, great Bugs Henderson, and of course, Stevie Ray Vaughan. As can be seen and heard, one of the main advantages of the composite blues scale is the prominent availability of more choice notes relative to the harmony of the I, V, and V chords. In particular, it encourages bends to the major 3rd (C♯) for the I chord (A7) and the ♭3rd (C), which functions as the ♭7th of the IV chord (D7). **Performance Tip:** Bend the B on string 3 at fret 4 in measures 1–4 with the ring finger backed up by the middle and index. Play the E note on string 2 at fret 5 in measures 1 and 2 with the pinky finger.

Fig. 50

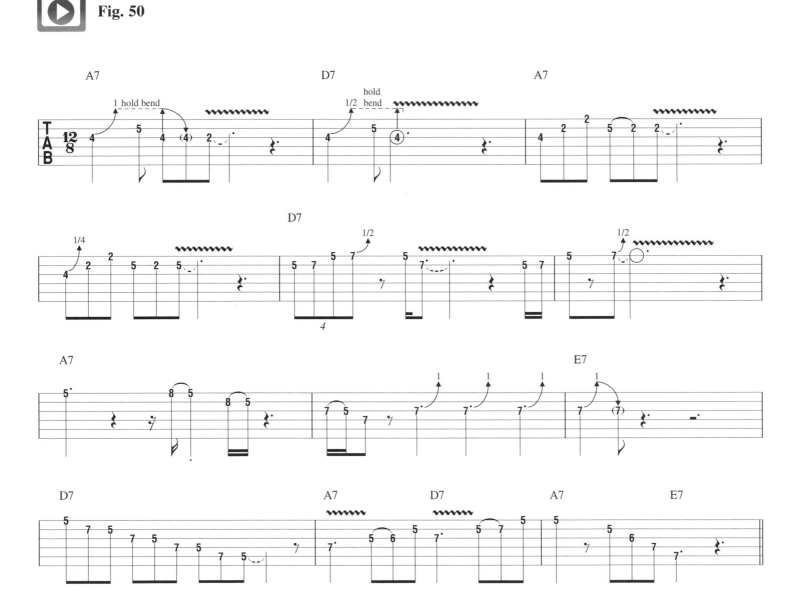

Allman Brothers Style

An especially fruitful approach to utilizing the composite blues scale, as played with stunning results by Duane Allman and Dickey Betts when paired as the "dynamic duo" in the Allman Brothers Band, is by going back and forth between it and the straight blues scale, as in **Fig. 51**. Measures 1–4 over the I chord, contrasted with measures 5–6 over the IV chord, bears this out. Hence, a good blues soloing strategy is to use the composite blues scale over the I chord, emphasizing the major 3rd (C♯), and the blues scale for the IV chord, emphasizing the ♭3rd (C), as per **Fig. 50**. **Performance Tip:** Access the triplets in measure 11 by barring strings 2 and 1 at fret 5 with the index finger and bending the D on string 3 at fret 7 with the ring finger, backed up by the middle finger.

 Fig. 51

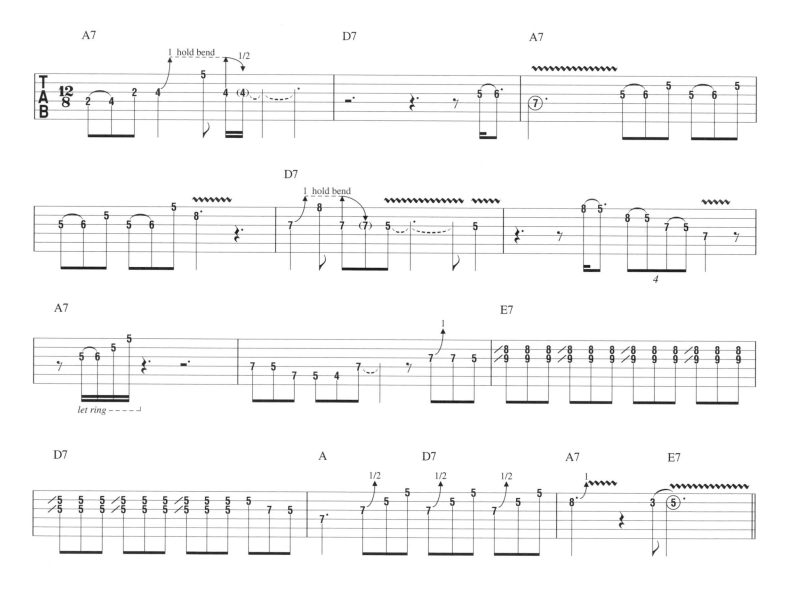

B.B. King Style

Fig. 52 combines the two scales in a manner that links the style of B.B. King to one of his prize protégés, Eric Clapton. As opposed to **Fig. 51**, the scales are mixed more freely while the licks are still chosen to complement the chord changes, as all blues solos should. **Performance Tip:** Play the repeating E note on string 1 in measure 5 with the ring finger, also employing it to bend the same note in measure 6.

Fig. 52

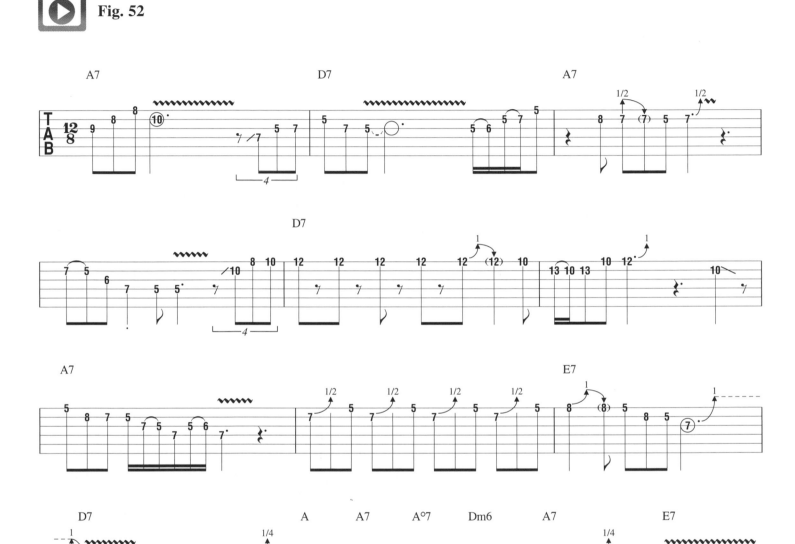

Chapter 9
Slippin' 'n' Slidin' – Introduction to Bottleneck Guitar

It has been said the alto saxophone most faithfully imitates the tonality of the human voice. However, bottleneck, or slide guitarists, may even more accurately reproduce the nuances, inflections, and melisma of vocalists due to the easy accessibility of microtones not as available with even bent fretted notes. The vast majority of blues slide guitarists play in open tunings like G and D, as we shall see, though Robert Nighthawk, Earl Hooker, and Mick Taylor are famed for "glissing" in standard.

Choosing a Slider

Prewar blues guitarists often literally used broken-off and smoothed bottlenecks to slip over their finger, usually after draining the contents of said wine or beer bottle. Bones and the edge of a pocket knife were also put into service. Nonetheless, virtually all contemporary guitarists play with a commercial brass, glass, steel, or ceramic slide. All produce differing tones and amounts of sustain, with the choice being entirely subjective and personal. **Performance Tip:** Though slide masters such as Duane Allman and Bonnie Raitt placed their slider on the middle finger, it is more efficient to place it on the pinky (like the prewar masters) in order to free up the other fingers for conventional fretting.

Basic Technique

Playing slide guitar requires totally different technique from conventional fretting. It is a challenge to acquire, but the resulting skill can add an extra expressive, emotional aspect to your playing, unobtainable in any other way. **Performance Tip:** Of utmost importance is the critical necessity of placing the slider *directly over* the desired fret wire for accurate intonation. Apply just enough pressure to extract a clean sound, *without* pressing the string down to the fret itself. Next, the muting of unwanted strings must be addressed by *lightly* dragging the pressed together index, middle, and ring fingers on the strings behind the slider. In addition, use the heel of the right hand palm to mute unwanted string noise in between picked notes.

Standard Tuning

An arrangement of *the* iconic slide riff from "Dust My Broom" appears in **Fig. 53**. The classic Elmore James version is in open D tuning, while this example resides in standard tuning in the key of E. **Performance Tip:** Muting in between each note is necessary in measure 6, as well as 9 and 10, to avoid unwanted dissonance, which can occur when moving diagonally between strings.

 Fig. 53

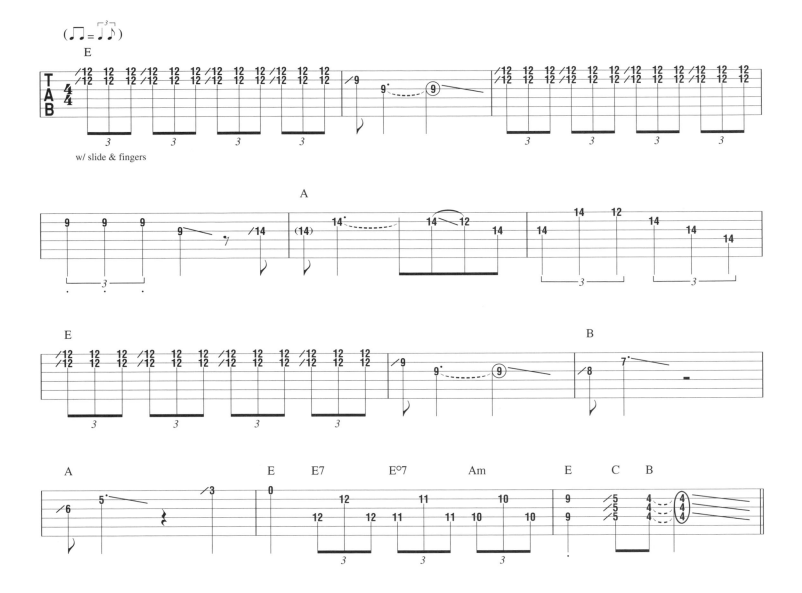

Open G Tuning

Open G is the most popular open tuning, finding adherents in rock, country, and folk music, besides the blues. Son House, Robert Johnson, and Muddy Waters employed it conspicuously in their recordings. As may be seen in the notation, open G consists of literally tuning to the notes of a G major chord with D–G–D–G–B–D, low to high. Close observation reveals strings 4, 3, and 2 to be the same pitch as standard tuning, making it a relatively simple tuning to understand and grasp. Likewise, it relates to open A chord-type barre chords with the root on string 5. Open A tuning, as used extensively by Robert Johnson, contains the same relative intervals as open G; it's only tuned up one step. **Fig. 54** is based on one of the oldest forms in the genre: the "walking blues." **Performance Tip:** Though obvious, be sure to lift your slider totally clear of the strings when moving from the B♭ note on string 5 at fret 3 to the G note on string 1 at fret 5. At the same time, be careful to not slap the slider down on the string.

▶ **Fig. 54**

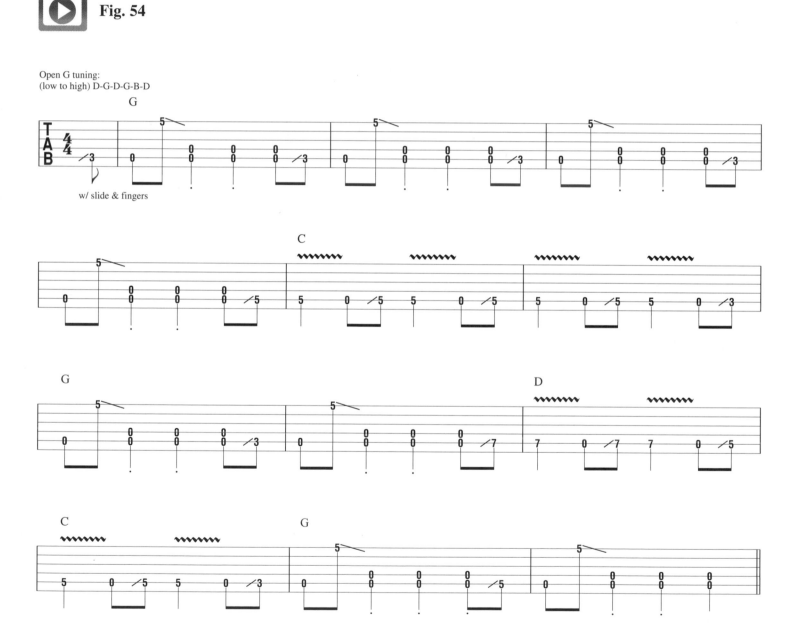

Fig. 55 shows one of the great advantages of open G tuning when it comes to creating chord-based riffs: Major barre chords may be accessed by simply placing the slider across all six strings at the desired fret position. Though similar to traditional patterns harking back to the prewar country blues era, the example also references Led Zeppelin's powerhouse, apocalyptic version of Memphis Minnie's "When the Levee Breaks." **Performance Tip:** Be sure to position the slide directly over the fret wires and don't push the strings down!

 **Fig. 55**

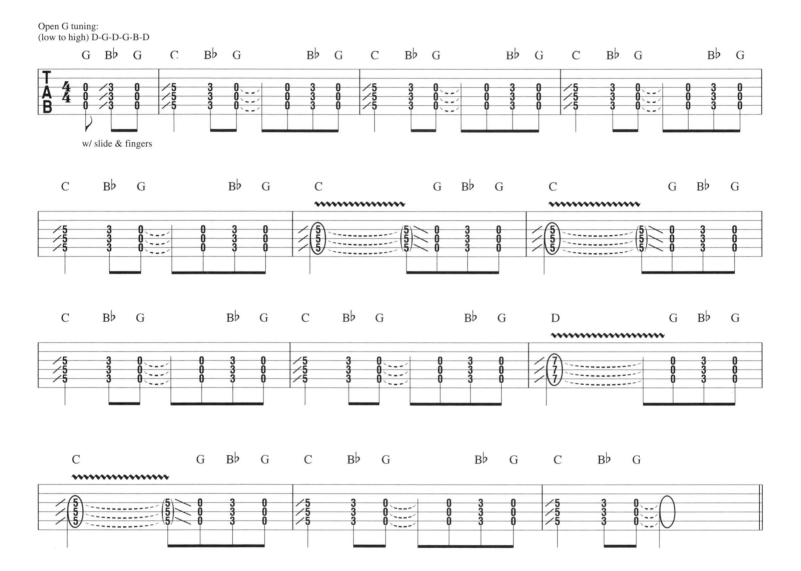

Open D Tuning

Open D tuning, consisting of D–A–D–F♯–A–D (low to high), may be perceived to have a darker, bluesier tonality than open G. Other potential advantages for guitarists only used to playing in standard tuning is the way it relates to open E chord-type barre chords with the root on string 6, as well as the fingering for the root position of the minor pentatonic or blues scale. **Performance Tip:** Open E tuning, as utilized by Robert Johnson, Duane Allman, and Derek Trucks, among others, contains the same relative intervals as open D but is tuned one step higher. **Figs. 56A** and **56B** contain the root position of the A minor pentatonic scale in standard tuning and the root position of an A major chord in open D combined with a few choice notes from the minor pentatonic scale, respectively. **Performance Tip:** Be sure to mute the strings between notes, particularly when incorporating the additional notes on string 6, 2, and 1.

Fig. 56A

A Minor Pentatonic Scale

5fr

Fig. 56B

Open D Tuning

7fr

Fig. 57 shines a light on several important attributes of open D tuning, including easy access to boogie patterns on strings 6 and 5 with the root on the bottom, as well as major triads on strings 3–1. In addition, it also contains a convenient open-position A7 (V) chord voicing as seen in measure 12. **Performance Tip:** Make a small barre on strings 6 and 5 with the index finger in measures 5 and 9. Finger the A7 voicing in measure 12 with the middle and index, low to high.

Fig. 57

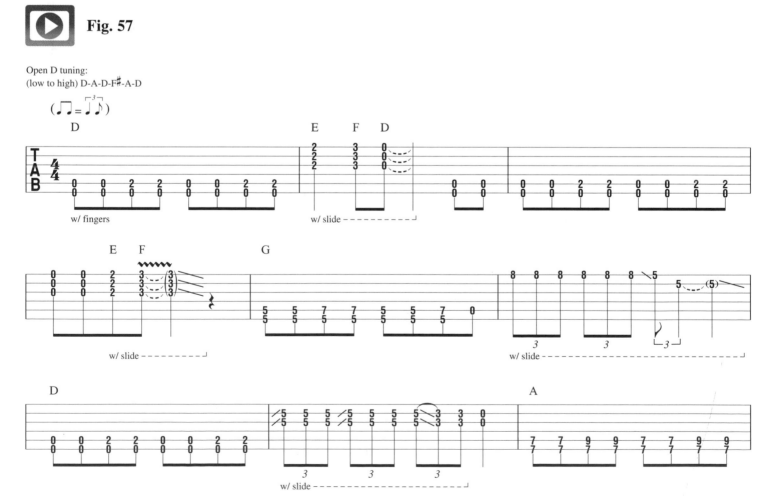

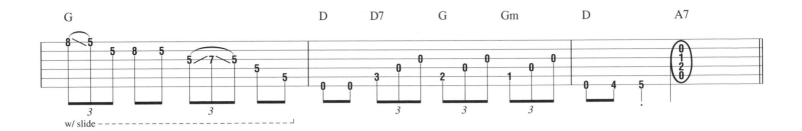

Fig. 58 harkens back to early country and Delta blues. Echoes of "Catfish Blues" and other prewar classics reverberate in the riffs of measures 1–4 and 7–8 over the I (D) chord. **Performance Tip:** Muting will be a constant requirement when jumping from string to string. Take note how the root positions for the IV (G) and V (A) chords reside at frets 5 and 7, respectively, in open D tuning, as in open G as well.

Fig. 58

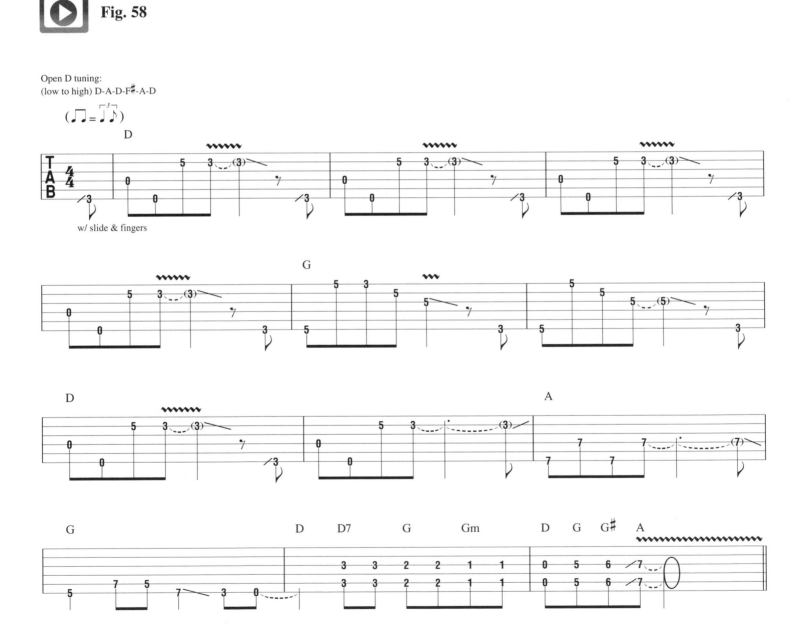

"Shake Your Moneymaker" by the acknowledged master of postwar open D tuning, Elmore "Elmo" James, is the basis for **Fig. 59**. Again, one of its main characteristics is readily apparent as the double stop, or *dyad*, on beat 1 of every measure contains the easily accessible major 3rd and 5th (low to high) of the I, IV, and V major chords, respectively. **Performance Tip:** Be careful to just strike strings 3 and 2 where indicated for the cleanest harmony.

 Fig. 59

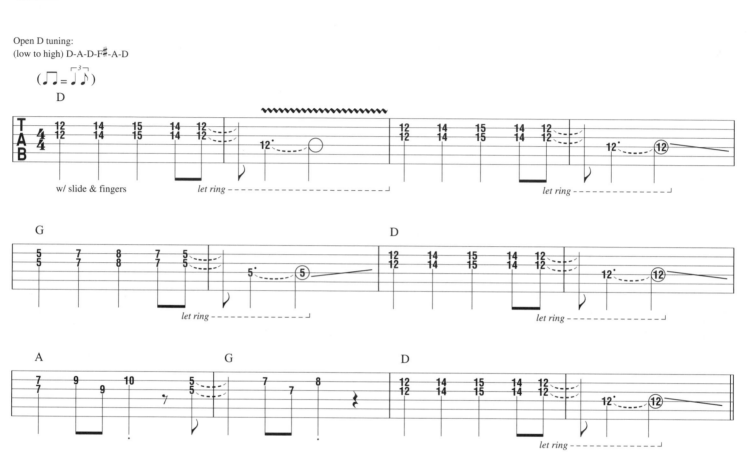

Chapter 10
The Blues Alone – Introduction to Solo Delta Blues

One of the oldest forms of recorded blues is the most challenging and, some would say, the most rewarding. Solo Delta acoustic or electric blues is the "blues alone" and can be the deepest and most emotionally expressive of all. Many are in open tunings, while the standard tuning examples shown are especially accessible and instructive.

Fingerstyle Technique

Though not an absolute prerequisite, fingerstyle technique is the most efficient for solo blues. Legends such as Mississippi John Hurt and the Rev. Gary Davis utilized only the thumb and index finger, while others opt for the index and middle fingers in conjunction with the thumb. It is a topic open to interpretation with no real right or wrong way, though it is recommended to use the thumb mostly for the three bass strings.

An option, especially for electric guitarists, is the *hybrid picking* method, where the pick is held between the thumb and index and employed for the bass strings, while the middle finger, and possibly the ring finger, access the treble strings. Another consideration is the use of a plastic thumbpick, which produces a louder, crisper bass-string tone than bare flesh.

Key of E

Fig. 60 in the key of E contains one of the foundation riffs of prewar blues in measures 1–4 and 7–8 over the I (E) chord. It appears in versions of "Catfish Blues" and in the early postwar electric blues of Muddy Waters' "Rollin' Stone." Additionally, measures 5–6 over the IV (A) chord show how the concept of "less is more" can produce a dynamic effect while still implying the A7 harmony. **Performance Tip:** Execute the quarter-step "blue-note" bend on string 6 in the I chord riff by pulling *down* with the middle finger. Similarly, bend the A note on string 3 by pulling down with the index finger.

 Fig. 60

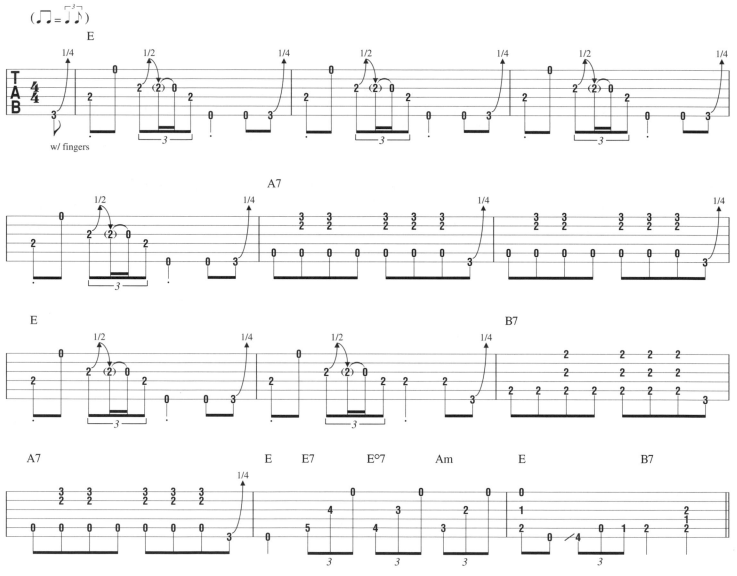

Key of A

The key of A appears frequently in Delta blues in addition to E. Measures 1–4 and 7–8 over the I (A) chord in **Fig. 61** contain a version of the classic I–I7 (A7) move found throughout prewar blues, such as in Robert Johnson's "Steady Rollin' Man" (1936). Both keys, of course, feature advantageous root-note open strings. The IV (D) chord in measures 5–6 also presents a classic IV7 chord as a first-inversion form with the 3rd (F♯) on the bottom, as opposed to the root (D). **Performance Tip:** Though not notated as such, it is suggested to make an A major barre-chord voicing with the index finger at fret 2 across strings 4–1. Follow with the pinky at fret 5 on string 1 and the middle finger at fret 3 to imply the A7 chord. As previously mentioned, employ the right-hand thumb on string 6. For the D7/F♯ chord, utilize the left-hand thumb for the F♯ note on string 6 and employ either the index, or index and middle together, to brush up on strings 3–1 at the same time. The run down the root position of the A minor pentatonic scale in measure 10 could be accomplished just with upstrokes of the index finger.

 Fig. 61

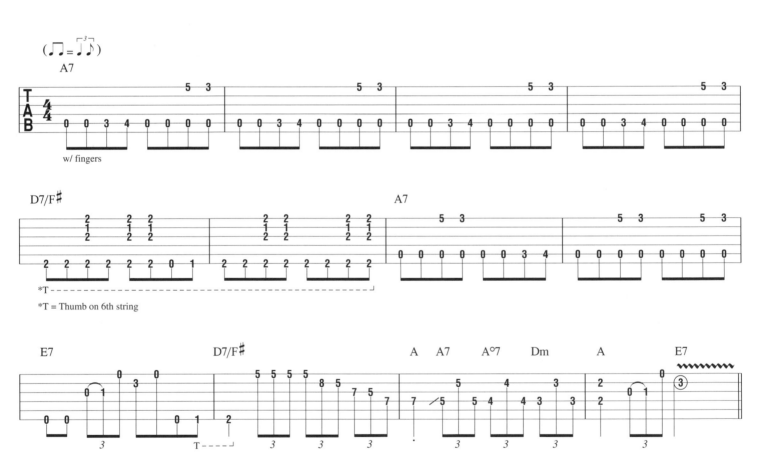

47

Key of D

Fig. 62 in the key of D is reminiscent of Tommy Johnson's classic "Big Road Blues." It is in standard tuning, as opposed to his version in drop D (in which the low E string is tuned down to D). As in E and A, D has its own special characteristics, including allowing the I (D), IV (G), and V (A) chord changes to be "voiced" with open-position chords. Most prominently, it offers the opportunity to walk up the low E string to F♯ (3rd), which implies a first-inversion D/F♯ chord. **Performance Tip:** In measures 1–4 and 7–8 over the I chord, play the chord tones with the middle and ring fingers while walking up string 6 with the thumb.

Fig. 62

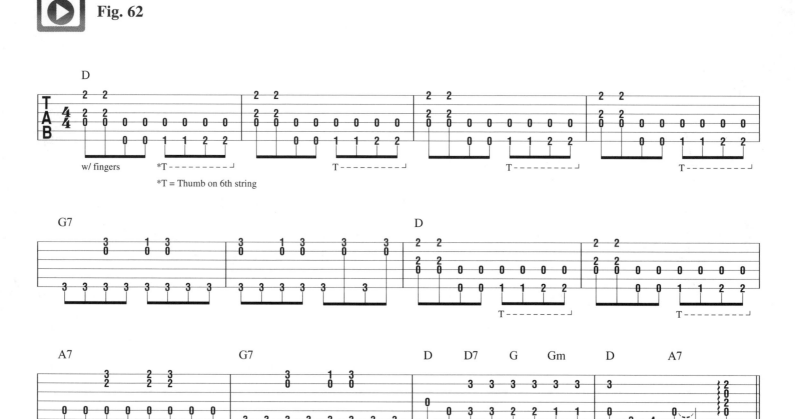